ANCIENT MYTHOLOGY
GREEK MYTHS AND LEGENDS

by Alyssa Krekelberg
illustrated by Cesar Samaniego

Tools for Parents & Teachers

Grasshopper Books enhance imagination and introduce the earliest readers to fun storylines and illustrations. The easy-to-read text supports early reading experiences with repetitive sentence patterns and sight words.

Before Reading
- Discuss the cover illustration. What do readers see?
- Look at the glossary together. Discuss the words.

During Reading
- "Walk" through the book with the reader. Discuss new or unfamiliar words. Sound them out together.
- Look at the illustrations. When and where does the story take place? What is happening in the story?

After Reading
- Prompt the child to think more. Ask: Which Greek myth or legend is your favorite? Why?

Grasshopper Books are published by Jump!
3500 American Blvd W, Suite 150
Bloomington, MN 55431
www.jumplibrary.com

Copyright © 2026 Jump! International copyright reserved in all countries. No part of this book may be reproduced in any form without written permission from the publisher.

Jump! is a division of FlutterBee Education Group.

Library of Congress Cataloging-in-Publication Data

Names: Krekelberg, Alyssa, author.
Samaniego, César, 1975- illustrator.
Title: Greek myths and legends / by Alyssa Krekelberg; illustrated by Cesar Samaniego.
Description: Minneapolis, MN: Jump!, Inc., [2026]
Series: Ancient mythology | Includes index.
Audience: Ages 7-10
Identifiers: LCCN 2024044358 (print)
LCCN 2024044359 (ebook)
ISBN 9798892137416 (hardcover)
ISBN 9798892137423 (paperback)
ISBN 9798892137430 (ebook)
Subjects: LCSH: Mythology, Greek—Juvenile literature. Gods, Greek—Juvenile literature. | Goddesses, Greek—Juvenile literature.
Classification: LCC BL783 .K74 2026 (print)
LCC BL783 (ebook)
DDC 398.20938—dc23/eng/20241206
LC record available at https://lccn.loc.gov/2024044358
LC ebook record available at https://lccn.loc.gov/2024044359

Editor: Katie Chanez
Direction and Layout: Anna Peterson
Illustrator: Cesar Samaniego
Content Consultant: Denise Demetriou, PhD; Professor of Ancient Greek History; University of California, San Diego

Printed in the United States of America at Corporate Graphics in North Mankato, Minnesota.

Table of Contents

On Mount Olympus	4
Greek Gods and Goddesses	22
To Learn More	23
Glossary	24
Index	24

On Mount Olympus

Zeus was king of the Greek gods. He lived high above the clouds on Mount Olympus. He was one of 12 gods and goddesses who lived there.

They each had special powers. Zeus was god of the sky. He could make and change the weather. He threw thunderbolts!

Ancient Greeks told stories about the gods and the heroes they helped. These stories are known as Greek **mythology**.

One of the oldest stories tells how Zeus became king. He and his siblings battled the **Titans** for 10 years. Each side wanted to rule the world.

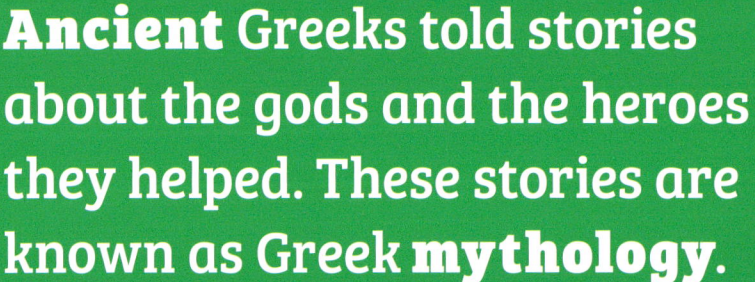

Zeus and his siblings won! Zeus became king. Hades became god of the **underworld**. Poseidon ruled the sea.

Poseidon and Athena both wanted a city named after them. They gave gifts to the people. Poseidon hit the ground with his trident. Water came out, but it was salty. People could not drink it.

Athena was very wise. She planted a seed. An olive tree grew. People used the tree's wood. They ate the olives and made olive oil. Athena gave the best gift! The city was named Athens after her.

Heracles was one of Zeus's sons. He was a hero. One day, the Hydra attacked him and his nephew, Iolaus. It had nine heads! Heracles cut one off. But two more grew. Heracles told Iolaus to touch the Hydra's neck with fire. The heads stopped growing. They beat the Hydra!

Hermes was the messenger god. One day, he flew to an island with a message from Zeus. The sea **nymph** Calypso had kept the hero Odysseus trapped on the island for seven years. Zeus wanted Odysseus to go home. Calypso was angry when Hermes told her. But she let Odysseus make a boat. He sailed home.

Odysseus

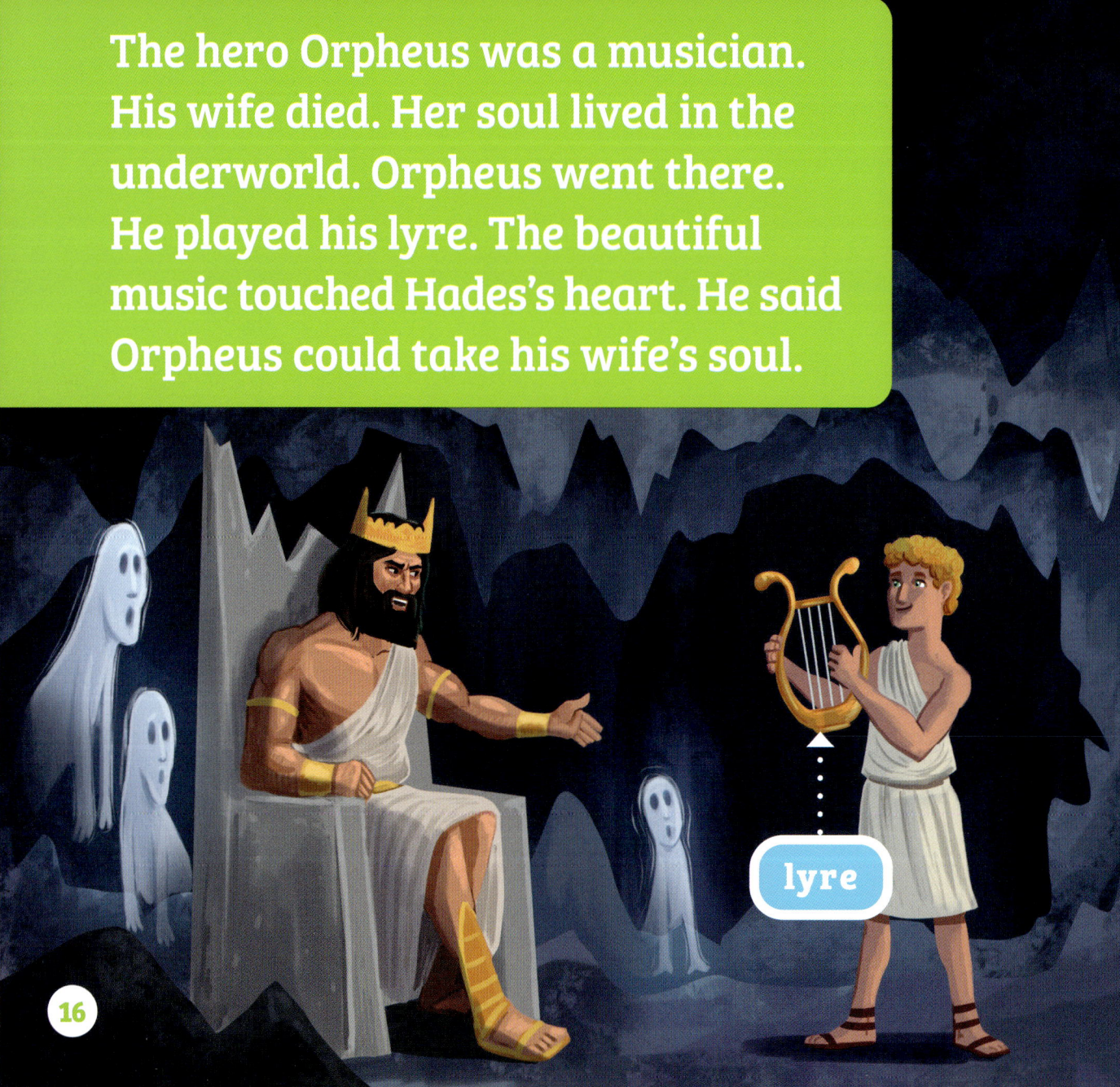

But there was one rule. Orpheus could not look at his wife. As he walked from the underworld, he could not hear her footsteps. Did Hades play a trick on him? Orpheus looked back. He saw his wife's soul. He broke Hades's rule! His wife faded away.

The hero Bellerophon wanted to catch a winged horse named Pegasus. Athena helped. She gave Bellerophon a gold **bridle**. Bellerophon snuck behind Pegasus. He slipped the bridle on him. He and Pegasus flew into the sky! They saved people from a fire-breathing Chimera.

One day, Zeus looked down from the clouds. People built him a **temple**. Zeus was happy with them. He sent rain to water their **crops**.

The gods could help or hurt people with their powers. On this day, Zeus helped!

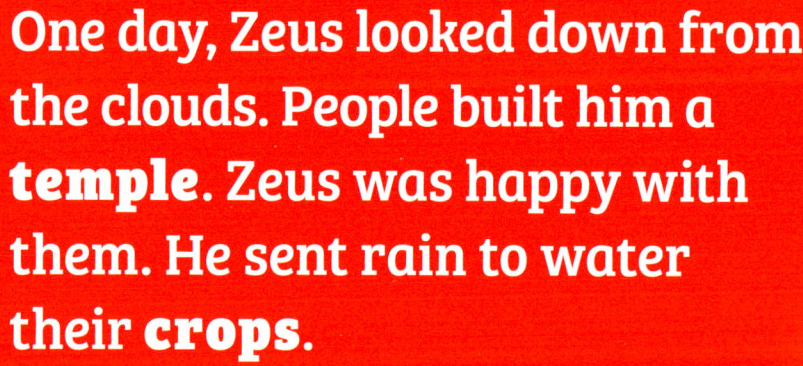

Greek Gods and Goddesses

Who are Greek mythology's most important gods and goddesses? Take a look!

Aphrodite
Goddess of love and beauty

Apollo
God of music, healing, and archery. He was the twin brother of Artemis.

Ares
God of war

Artemis
Goddess of wild animals, hunting, and childbirth. She was the twin sister of Apollo.

Athena
Goddess of war and wisdom

Demeter
Goddess of farming

Dionysus
God of plants

Hades
God of the underworld

Hephaestus
God of fire

Hera
Goddess of marriage and women. She was Zeus's wife.

Hermes
Messenger god

Hestia
Goddess of the home

Poseidon
God of the sea

Zeus
King of the gods and god of the sky

To Learn More

Finding more information is as easy as 1, 2, 3.
❶ Go to www.factsurfer.com
❷ Enter "**Greekmythsandlegends**" into the search box.
❸ Choose your book to see a list of websites.

Glossary

ancient: Very old or from the very distant past.
bridle: A harness that fits around a horse's head and is used to guide or control the horse.
crops: Plants grown for food.
mythology: A group of stories from a particular culture or religion.
nymph: A female goddess who lived in nature, such as the sea or forest.
temple: A building in which a god is worshipped.
Titans: Giants who ruled Earth before the Olympian gods.
underworld: A place in myths where the dead go.

Index

Athena 10, 11, 18
Athens 11
Calypso 14
Chimera 18
Hades 8, 16, 17
Heracles 12
Hermes 14
Hydra 12
Iolaus 12
Mount Olympus 4
Odysseus 14
Pegasus 18
Poseidon 8, 10
Titans 6
underworld 8, 16, 17
Zeus 4, 5, 6, 8, 12, 14, 20